DEC 2002

S0-AHV-167

Alameda County
LIBRARY
...Infinite possibilities

Opening Day Collection 2003
Purchased with funds from the City of Dublin

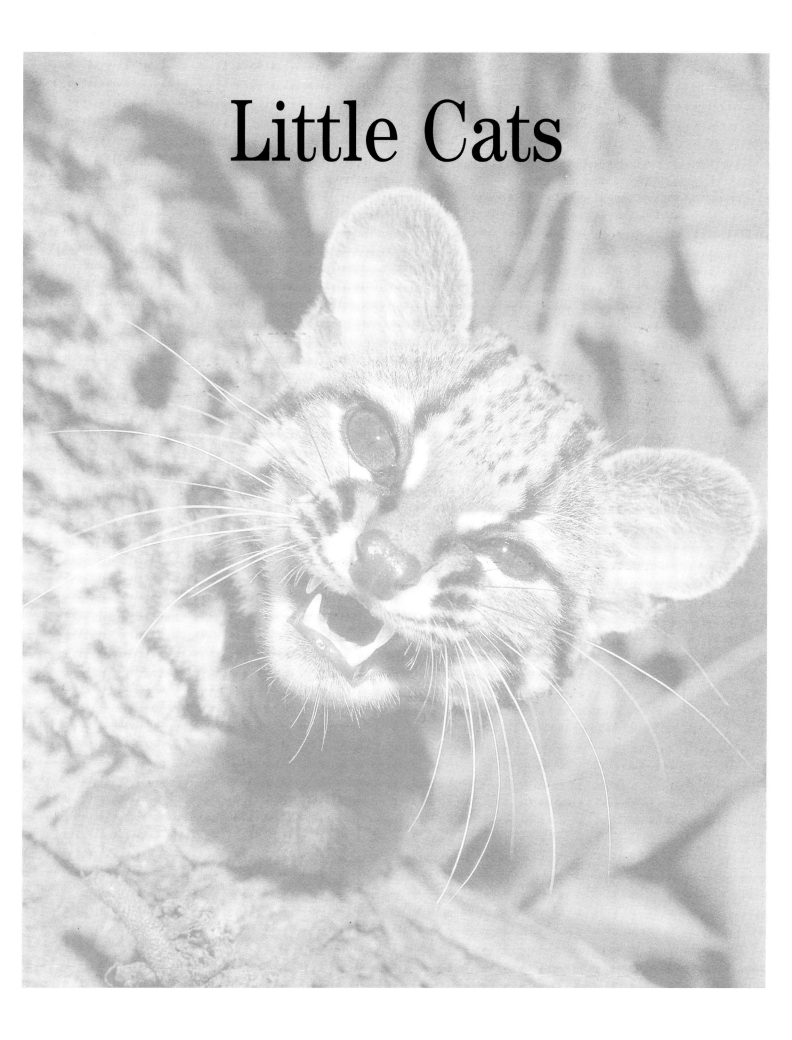

Little Cats

Published by Wildlife Education, Ltd.
12233 Thatcher Court, Poway, California 92064
contact us at: 1-800-477-5034
e-mail at: animals@zoobooks.com
visit us at: www.zoobooks.com

Copyright © 2000 hardbound edition by Wildlife Education, Ltd.
All rights reserved. No part of this book may be reproduced in any form without written permission from the publisher.
Printed in U.S.A.

ISBN 0-937934-82-8

Little Cats

Created and Written by
John Bonnett Wexo

Scientific Consultants
Dennis A. Meritt, Jr., Ph.D.
Director of Collections, Retired
Lincoln Park Zoo

Edward C. Schmitt
Former General Curator
Denver Zoo

Art Credits

Pages Eight and Nine: Richard Orr

Pages Ten and Eleven: Richard Orr

Pages Twelve and Thirteen: Richard Orr

Page Twelve: Top Right, Walter Stuart

Page Thirteen: Top Left, Walter Stuart

Pages Sixteen and Seventeen: Richard Orr

Page Seventeen: Middle Right, Walter Stuart

Pages Twenty and Twenty-one: Richard Orr

Page Twenty: Top Right, Walter Stuart

Page Twenty-one: Top Right, Walter Stuart

Photographic Credits

Cover: Francois Gohier

Pages Six and Seven: M.J. Griffith *(Photo Researchers)*

Page Ten: Lynn Rogers

Page Twelve: Hans Reinhard *(Bruce Coleman, Ltd.)*

Pages Fourteen and Fifteen: Breck P. Kent *(Animals Animals)*

Pages Sixteen and Seventeen: Top, Hans Reinhard *(Bruce Coleman, Inc.)*

Page Sixteen: Tom McHugh *(Photo Researchers)*

Page Seventeen: Stephen Krasemann *(DRK)*

Pages Eighteen and Nineteen: Stephen J. Krasemann *(Photo Researchers)*

Page Twenty-one: Left, Jane Howard *(Photo Researchers)*; Left Center, Jeff Lepore *(Photo Researchers)*; Right Center, Tom and Pat Leeson *(Photo Researchers)*; Right, Margot Conte *(Animals Animals)*

Pages Twenty-two and Twenty-three: Marty Stouffer *(Animals Animals)*

Cover Photo: A Margay

Our Thanks To: Lida Burney; Dr. Oliver Ryder *(San Diego Zoo)*; San Diego Zoo Library Staff; Dr. Bill Newman and Dr. Fleminger *(Scripps Institution of Oceanography)*; and Lynnette Wexo.

Contents

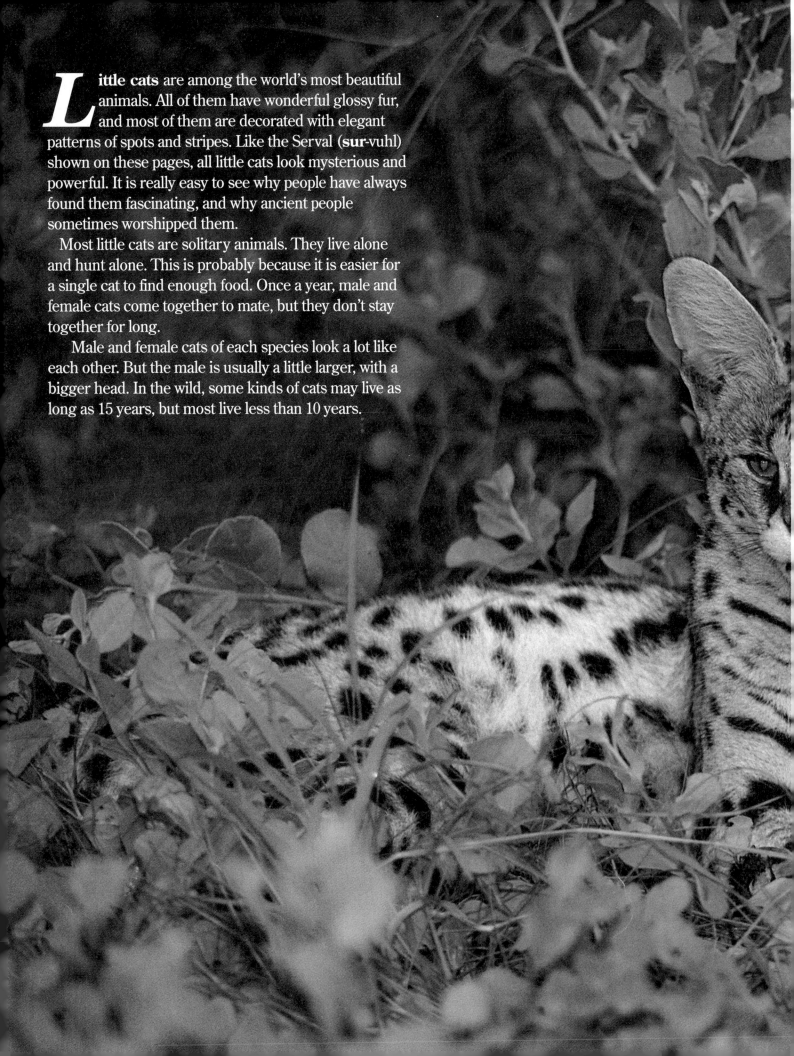

Little cats are among the world's most beautiful animals. All of them have wonderful glossy fur, and most of them are decorated with elegant patterns of spots and stripes. Like the Serval (**sur**-vuhl) shown on these pages, all little cats look mysterious and powerful. It is really easy to see why people have always found them fascinating, and why ancient people sometimes worshipped them.

Most little cats are solitary animals. They live alone and hunt alone. This is probably because it is easier for a single cat to find enough food. Once a year, male and female cats come together to mate, but they don't stay together for long.

Male and female cats of each species look a lot like each other. But the male is usually a little larger, with a bigger head. In the wild, some kinds of cats may live as long as 15 years, but most live less than 10 years.

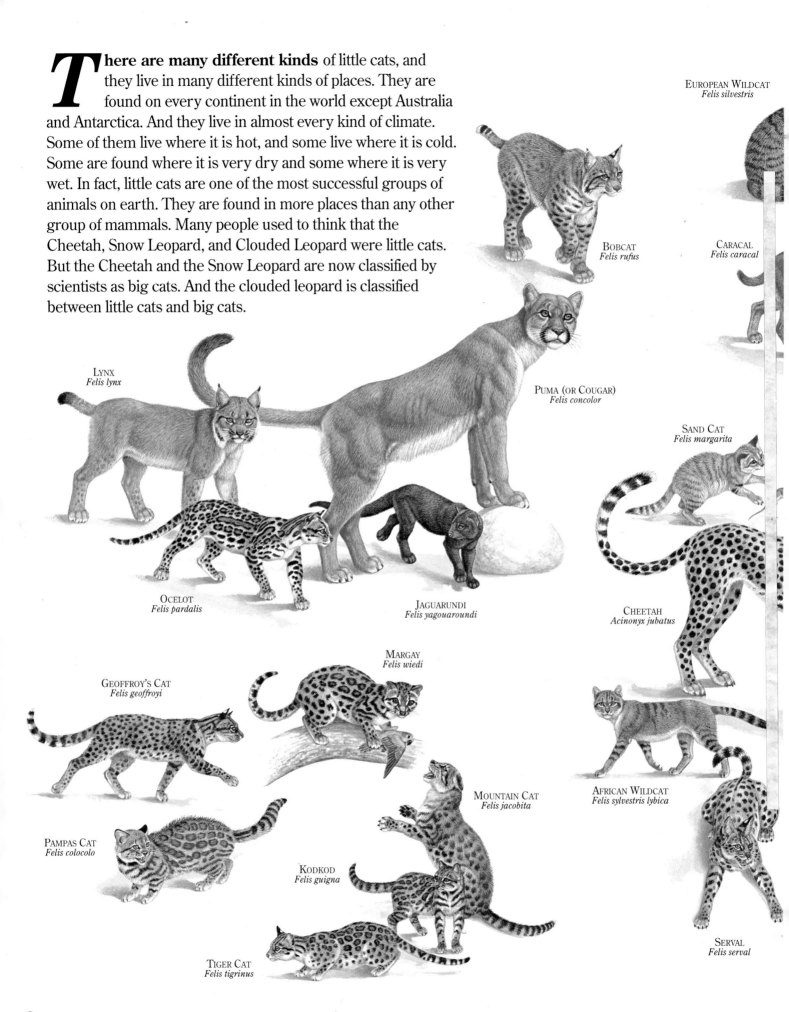

There are many different kinds of little cats, and they live in many different kinds of places. They are found on every continent in the world except Australia and Antarctica. And they live in almost every kind of climate. Some of them live where it is hot, and some live where it is cold. Some are found where it is very dry and some where it is very wet. In fact, little cats are one of the most successful groups of animals on earth. They are found in more places than any other group of mammals. Many people used to think that the Cheetah, Snow Leopard, and Clouded Leopard were little cats. But the Cheetah and the Snow Leopard are now classified by scientists as big cats. And the clouded leopard is classified between little cats and big cats.

EUROPEAN WILDCAT
Felis silvestris

BOBCAT
Felis rufus

CARACAL
Felis caracal

LYNX
Felis lynx

PUMA (OR COUGAR)
Felis concolor

SAND CAT
Felis margarita

OCELOT
Felis pardalis

JAGUARUNDI
Felis yagouaroundi

CHEETAH
Acinonyx jubatus

MARGAY
Felis wiedi

GEOFFROY'S CAT
Felis geoffroyi

MOUNTAIN CAT
Felis jacobita

AFRICAN WILDCAT
Felis sylvestris lybica

PAMPAS CAT
Felis colocolo

KODKOD
Felis guigna

TIGER CAT
Felis tigrinus

SERVAL
Felis serval

PALLAS'S CAT
Felis manul

SNOW LEOPARD
Panthera uncia

CHINESE DESERT CAT
Felis bieti

IRIOMOTE CAT
Felis iriomotensis

ASIATIC STEPPE CAT
Felis sylvestris ornata

LEOPARD CAT
Felis bengalensis

TEMMINCK'S GOLDEN CAT
Felis temmincki

FISHING CAT
Felis viverrina

JUNGLE CAT (OR REED CAT)
Felis chaus

RUSTY-SPOTTED CAT
Felis rubiginosus

AFRICAN GOLDEN CAT
Felis aurata

CLOUDED LEOPARD
Neofelis nebulosa

FLAT-HEADED CAT
Felis planiceps

BLACK-FOOTED CAT
Felis nigripes

BAY CAT (OR BORNEAN RED CAT)
Felis badia

MARBLED CAT
Felis marmorata

*H*ow do you tell a "little" cat from a "big" cat? Strange as it may seem, scientists have had a hard time answering this question. You might think that a "little" cat is simply a cat that is little. But it is not that simple. Some little cats are very large. And a few of them are larger than some "big" cats, as you will see below.

You might think that big cats would do things in a bigger way than little cats. But this isn't always true, either. Some little cats can jump longer distances than big cats. In general, little cats are also as good at hunting as big cats.

Scientists used to think there was one thing that was always different between "big" cats and "little" cats. They thought that all big cats could roar and that all little cats could not roar. It is still true that all cats called little cats cannot roar. But now, some cats that cannot roar have been included in the group of big cats—the Cheetah, Snow Leopard, and Clouded Leopard. It's all a bit confusing.

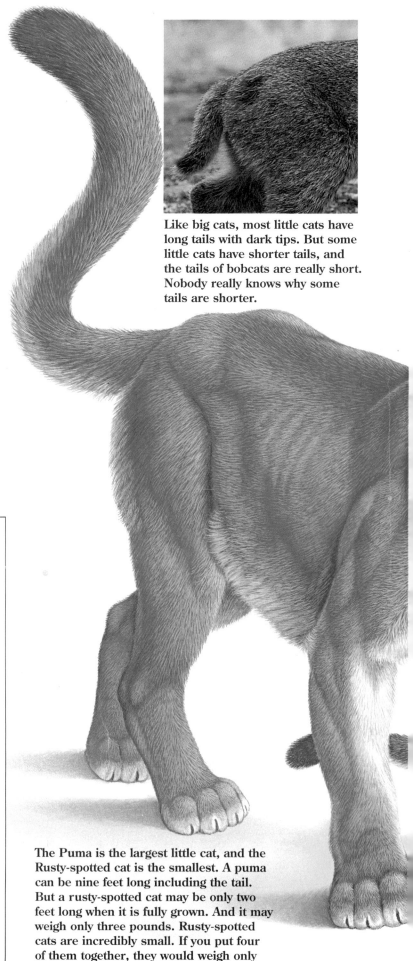

Like big cats, most little cats have long tails with dark tips. But some little cats have shorter tails, and the tails of bobcats are really short. Nobody really knows why some tails are shorter.

LEOPARD

The Leopard is called a "big" cat. But some "little" cats are bigger than some leopards. The largest known leopard weighed 233 pounds.

PUMA

But the largest puma ever weighed was more than *300 pounds.*

The Puma is the largest little cat, and the Rusty-spotted cat is the smallest. A puma can be nine feet long including the tail. But a rusty-spotted cat may be only two feet long when it is fully grown. And it may weigh only three pounds. Rusty-spotted cats are incredibly small. If you put four of them together, they would weigh only as much as one average house cat.

10

The Snow Leopard is the best jumper of the big cats. But a Puma—a little cat—can jump almost as far as a Snow Leopard. A Puma was once seen jumping 18 feet *straight up* into a tree. That's as high as the top of a two-story building!

SNOW LEOPARD—49 FEET

PUMA—40 FEET

The eyes of most little cats are different from the eyes of big cats. When bright light shines on the eye of a little cat, the pupil closes to a slit **1**. But the pupil of a big cat's eye closes to a circle **2**.

RUSTY-SPOTTED CAT

Little cats can't roar, because they have a different kind of voice box from big cats. There is a series of bones inside the voice box of a little cat **3**. The bones are connected so tightly that they cannot vibrate very much. They can only make small vibrations, and these produce small sounds. Most big cats have a cord in their voice boxes **4** that can vibrate more and make bigger sounds.

purrrrrrrrr(

ROAR!!

Cats are wonderful hunters. Almost every part of a cat's body has something to do with finding prey, catching it, or eating it. For example, some cats are covered with spots or stripes, because this makes it harder to see them when they hide in trees or bushes. Other cats have plain coats that make them hard to see when they hide in grass. In both cases, the coat helps the cats get very close to their prey before they attack, as shown on the opposite page.

All little cats are meat eaters. But different species eat different kinds of meat. Some cats eat things as small as a mouse, while a few catch prey as big as a zebra. Others eat birds, lizards, frogs, fish, and even large insects. In many places, little cats are helpful to people, because they kill rodents and other animals that destroy human crops.

Most little cats hunt at night, and they have special equipment to help them find prey in the dark. A few little cats hunt during the day.

To cut meat, cats have special teeth that are very different from your teeth. Humans have cheek teeth that are flat and wide like pliers. These are used for grinding food. The cheek teeth of cats are narrow and sharp like scissors.

To hunt at night, cats need eyes that can see in the dark. Like owls, they have big eyes that are very sensitive to light. Most cats can actually see *six times better* than people can in the dark. They are particularly good at seeing animals that are moving around. If an animal stays very still, a cat may not see it.

Cats also need good hearing to help them catch prey. In a dense forest or in thick grass, they may hear prey coming long before they can see it. Unlike humans, cats don't have to move their heads to know what direction a sound is coming from. They just move their ears.

Whiskers help cats to find their way in the dark. The whiskers are sensitive, like the ends of your fingers. Cats can push their whiskers out in front of them to feel their way along—just like you may put your fingers out to feel your way in a dark room.

EUROPEAN WILDCAT

Most wild cats and house cats catch their food in the same way. They sneak up on their prey, trying to get as close as they can without being seen. This is called stalking (stawk-ing). The closer the cat gets to its prey, the slower it moves. It stays close to the ground. And it hides behind bushes and rocks to keep the prey from seeing it ①.

1

When the cat gets very close to its prey, it doesn't attack right away. Instead, it flattens itself against the ground and watches the prey for a while ②.

2

CARACAL

After watching the prey for some time, the cat suddenly rushes forward. It tries to knock the prey over with its paws ③.

3

Even though cats are very good hunters, they don't always catch the animals they go after. In fact, most cats have to stalk 10 to 20 animals before they actually catch one. Of all animals, birds are the hardest to catch. They usually fly away before the cat even gets near them.

13

PUMA (COUGAR)

Size can help an animal conserve body heat. A large, round body stays warm much longer than a small one. That is why a puma in Alaska is much larger than a puma found in an Amazon jungle. This animal is from southern Canada.

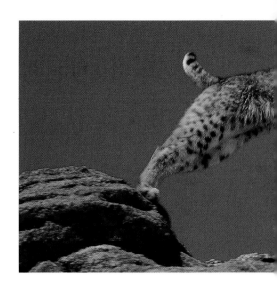

Cats can move with a grace and agility that is wonderful to watch. All little cats have very flexible bodies and an excellent sense of balance. And for these reasons, they can move in ways that seem next to impossible.

Most cats can walk so silently that nobody can hear them coming. Some can climb trees in the twinkling of an eye. And others can leap through the air so lightly that they almost seem to be flying.

All of this marvelous movement helps cats to hunt, of course. It helps them to chase prey up a tree if necessary. And it allows them to surprise prey on the ground by leaping down from a tree.

The best climber of all little cats is probably the Margay. This beautiful animal has very flexible feet that can be hooked over a branch like hands. Just for the fun of it, a margay may hang upside down by one foot.

Most cats have soft pads on the bottom of their feet to help them walk quietly. And some cats have feet that are special in other ways as well. Sand Cats live in the desert, and they have thick mats of hair on the bottom of their feet. The mats protect the feet from the hot sand. The Lynx (lingks) lives in the north and has to walk on snow. It has broad feet that spread the weight of the cat like snowshoes. The wide feet keep a lynx from sinking too deeply into the snow, as shown below.

The best climber among the big cats is probably the Clouded Leopard. Clouded Leopards do most of their hunting in trees and can run up and down tree trunks like squirrels.

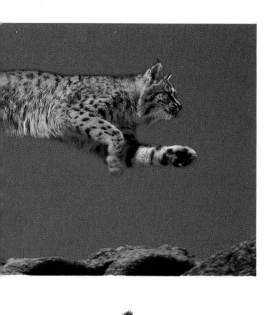

Many little cats are good jumpers, and jumping often helps them catch their prey. In wooded areas, bobcats like to sneak up on their prey, but in deserts and rocky country, this is difficult. Here, a bobcat might make a brief rush toward an animal before taking one big leap to land on its prey. Bobcats can jump seven or eight feet with no trouble at all.

Claws help cats to grip the ground as they run and climb. Most cats have claws that can be pulled back into the foot when they are not being used. A muscle is attached to the top of each claw. When the muscle pulls①, the claw moves up and back②.

Another muscle is attached to the bottom of the claw. When this muscle is pulled back ③, the claw moves down and forward④. Cats bring their claws out when they are attacking prey, to help them grab the prey and hold on to it.

Most people think that all cats hate to go into the water, but this isn't true. Some little cats go swimming all the time. And a few cats catch most of their food in the water. The best swimmer of all is the Fishing Cat. This cat usually stays by the side of a stream, grabbing fish with its paws. But sometimes, it will leap right into the water and swim to the bottom, looking for crayfish and other good things to eat. The Fishing Cat even has webs between the toes of its front feet to help it swim.

17

The ancestor of all house cats was probably the African Wildcat. Most wild cats cannot be trained to live with people as domestic animals. But African wildcats can be very friendly to people and were probably easy to train.

Most scientists believe that African wildcats were first turned into domestic cats in Egypt, about 4,000 years ago. Since that time, people have taken domestic cats with them to many parts of the world, and cat lovers have developed many breeds of cats. Today, there are more than 500 million domestic cats in the world, with 33 different breeds.

The various breeds look very different from each other, with many different hair patterns and colors. But under the skin, they all look very much like African wildcats. And no matter how tame they may seem, they still behave like wild cats at times.

After cats were domesticated in Egypt, it took a long time for them to spread to other countries. It took about 1,600 years before the first domestic cats reached Rome. About 600 years after that, domestic cats were known in England. The first domestic cat to come to America probably sailed there on a ship with Christopher Columbus in the year 1492.

SPHYNX

ABYSSINIAN

AMERICAN SHORTHAIR

HAVANA BROWN

JAPANESE BOBTAIL

KORAT

LAVENDER

MAINE COON

SIAMESE

SOMALI

CHARTREUX

RAGDOLL

AFRICAN WILDCAT

SCOTTISH FOLD

HIMALAYAN

Egyptians worshipped cats as gods. It was a crime to hurt a cat, and anybody who did was put to death. It was also a crime to take cats out of Egypt. And this is probably why it took so long for domestic cats to spread to other countries. The cats had to be smuggled out of the country, as shown at right. Can you find the cat in the cartoon?

Wild cats sometimes mark their territories by scratching on trees. This is to warn other cats to stay away. At other times, wild cats may scratch on trees to sharpen their claws. Domestic cats scratch furniture for the same reasons. From the cat's point of view, the house it lives in is its territory. And the people who think they own the cat are really just guests in the cat's territory.

Many things that are done by domestic cats show that they still have a lot of wild cat in them. For instance, domestic cat mothers carry their babies around in the same way that wild cat mothers do.

BRITISH SHORTHAIR

TONKINESE

EGYPTIAN MAU

TURKISH ANGORA

MANX

BURMESE

BOMBAY

RUSSIAN BLUE

BALINESE

REX

BIRMAN

PERSIAN

21

The future of little cats is uncertain. Like many other kinds of wild animals, cats are in trouble today because some people are doing things that are very harmful to them. If we can convince such people to change their ways, the little cats will have a better chance to survive on this earth.

People can hurt cats in three major ways. First, there are people who kill some of the most beautiful cats to make coats out of their spotted and striped skins. Most of us, of course, feel that these skins are more beautiful when they are left on a living animal.

Some people kill wild cats to keep them from preying on farm animals, such as chickens and other small livestock. But cats often make up for the livestock they eat by killing many animals, such as rats and mice, that destroy human crops. The value of crops that cats save in this way is far greater than the value of the livestock the cats may eat.

Finally, some people harm little cats by taking away their habitats—the land the cats need to live on. More and more land is taken to build farms, factories, and houses on it. And in many places, this leaves no room for wild cats.

If we want to have little cats in this world, we must convince people to stop making coats out of their skins. We must help people to understand the good that cats do for ranchers and farmers. And we must make sure that there will always be enough wild places in which cats can live.

The best place for a wild cat is in its own unspoiled habitat, running free.

Index